Osterley Park and House

MIDDLESEX

A souvenir guide

THE NATIONAL TRUST

Above The Drawing Room ceiling

Below The West Front

AN 18TH-CENTURY PARTY PALACE

A mere eight miles from Piccadilly Circus lies a grand Neo-classical palace, set in an idealised landscape. Osterley Park is an astonishing survival, an 18th-century country estate on the western flank of London. Despite the encroachments of the last century, the park remains one of the largest open spaces in West London, and is much valued by people living locally.

THE GENIUS OF ADAM

Osterley Park House as we see it today was created in the late 18th century from a Tudor mansion. In the service of two extremely wealthy brothers, Francis and Robert Child, the architect Robert Adam (1728–92) spent two decades from 1761 designing and refining the house in imitation of classical antiquity. The result is an exercise in total design, with every aspect of the state rooms controlled by Adam.

The interior is one of the finest and most complete by Adam still in existence, and a testimony to his creative genius. It is full of delicate decorations designed by him and executed by his skilled assistants, with low reliefs, friezes and painted ornament. In addition, the rooms contain almost all of the original furniture designed by the architect specifically for each setting, often produced by the accomplished furniture-maker John Linnell (d.1796).

'Robert Child Esq .... rebuilt the Shell, ornamented, beautified, and new furnished the whole, in a Style of Elegance and Magnificence, that evince at once both his Taste and Liberality...'

W. Watts, *Seats of the Nobility and Gentry*, 1779

THE CHILD FAMILY

The Child family were successful bankers, originally from Wiltshire. Their wealth and social advancement began with goldsmithing in the City of London. They had strong interests in the East India Company and were much involved in trade as well as banking.

In the early 18th century, many prominent families moved to the west of London, as the prevailing winds meant that west London was less succeptible to the smoke and smells of the City. Osterley Park came into the possession of Sir Francis Child the Elder, former Lord Mayor of London, in 1713, having lain empty since 1698, when its previous owner, Nicholas Barbon, had died without repaying an outstanding mortgage on the property. Sir Francis already owned a house in Lincoln's Inn Fields, and the Child family used their villa at Osterley as a setting for fashionable socialising. It was their country estate, yet situated conveniently close to their business premises in the City of London.

The two brothers predominantly responsible for the redesign of Osterley Park, Francis and Robert, were brought up there and both used Osterley to entertain and impress their guests. In 1767 Robert sold the house in Lincoln's Inn Fields in order to buy 38 Berkeley Square from the Duke of Manchester. He engaged Robert Adam to redesign his new townhouse as well as Osterley, which their neighbour, Horace Walpole, called their 'palace *sans* coronet'.

Above The Tapestry Room fireplace

Far left Francis Child the Younger
Left Robert Child

Little changed in two centuries
The principal rooms are shown much as they were in 1782, shortly after Adam had completed his work on the house.

Above Robert Adam, who created the house we see today

'Adam the Scotch architect, who was principally employed on the alterations and improvements of Osterley, has seldom succeeded anywhere better, though he mixed, or left, or was obliged to leave some considerable faults.'

Horace Walpole, 1795

THE TUDOR HOUSE

In the 1570s the Tudor financier Sir Thomas Gresham had a rectangular manor house, 'faire and stately', built of brick to replace an older farmhouse at Osterley. It was laid out around a central courtyard with a turret at each corner. Osterley as it is today largely follows the 'footprint' of the Elizabethan house, and incorporates some of the original structure, aspects of which can be seen in the servants' quarters on the ground floor.

OSTERLEY TRANSFORMED

The house had become dilapidated, and so in the middle of the 18th century Francis Child engaged Robert Adam to remodel the buildings. Adam wanted to demolish the east front and reduce the north and south façades to the same size as that on the west. The proposal proved too radical, and instead he was asked to build a magnificent 'transparent' pillared portico complete with a pediment. Adam started work on Osterley in 1761 – his last design, for the Yellow Taffeta Bed, is dated 1779. Many of Adam's drawings for the house survive in the Soane Museum, making it a fascinating study in his progression as an architect from early robustness to later delicacy and subtlety.

Below The 'transparent' portico

REDISCOVERING ROME

Robert Adam was one of the most accomplished and influential architects in British history, and his work was to achieve fame throughout western Europe and North America. The interior schemes at Osterley are highly evolved and cosmopolitan, including references from the latest discoveries about the 'antique' world of ancient Rome.

Adam's inspiration came from a four-year study tour of European architecture in 1754–8. He returned with hundreds of drawings, many of which were reproduced in his book *Ruins of the Palace of the Emperor Diocletian at Spalatro* in 1764. Working with his brother James from a studio in London, he soon began to get commissions from wealthy and well-connected clients, many of whom would have been familiar with the latest findings about the ancient world.

TOTAL DESIGN

Adam was one of the earliest practitioners of 'total design'. Not only would he specify the interior decoration of each room, he would often design every detail of its contents, from the furniture to the light fittings, the bell-pull to the carpet. He pioneered the Neo-classical style – a delicate blend of primarily Greek and Roman sources. In his interior design, geometric schemes of great sophistication divide and marshal space, through the reproduction of architectural elements such as pillars and panels, ovals and circles. Typical motifs employed by Adam were vases, urns, vines, sphinxes and griffins, which were linked together by carefully rendered swags or ribbons. In addition, he designed appealing colour schemes of great subtlety. He defined his style as 'directed but not cramped by antiquity'.

A foreign finishing school

The Grand Tour was the equivalent of a finishing school for aristocratic youths. Accompanied usually by an older (and, hopefully, wiser) tutor, a trusted servant or two and plenty of funds, the young gentleman would embark upon a trip around Europe, taking in the great cities of Italy and visiting classical sites such as Pompeii, where archaeologists were unearthing the art and artefacts of the past. The English *milords* were avid collectors of classical antiquities, both genuine and copied, which they would have shipped back home to display in Neo-classical galleries or smaller cabinet rooms.

Below The excavations at Pompeii

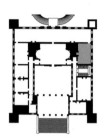

TOUR OF THE HOUSE

THE EATING ROOM

Here the Child family would entertain their guests at dinner. Almost every aspect of the room was designed by Robert Adam. The **ceiling** was installed first; it is decorated with grape vines, wine ewers and other symbols appropriate to hospitality and food. Celebratory scenes feature in the painted roundels within the ornate **stucco panels on the walls**, ranging from a Roman marriage to a wedding feast. Above the sideboard is a large painting by Antonio Zucchi (1726–95), *Turkish figures dancing among classical ruins. An offering to Ceres* by G.B. Cipriani (1727–85) hangs over the chimneypiece. Adam often employed Zucchi and Cipriani to supply painted decoration for his interiors.

Right The sideboard and dining chairs were placed against the walls. Temporary tables were brought in and set up at mealtimes

Opposite The stucco wall decoration had a practical purpose: it did not retain the smell of stale food

Furniture

To modern eyes, the room appears highly ornate, yet comparatively unfurnished. However, in the 18th century, gate-leg tables were stored in the adjoining corridor and brought in and set up for meals as required. Twelve *mahogany chairs* with lyre backs and two *armchairs* are placed against the walls, as they would have been when not in use.

Adam's magnificent carved and gilt *mahogany sideboard*, designed in 1767, was a permanent fixture, and had a very large silver wine-cooler underneath, an impressive indication of the family's wealth. A pair of white painted and gilt pedestals supports carved mahogany vases on either side of the sideboard. One is lined with lead so that it could be used to hold ice or water. The pedestals can be opened; one would have contained a mahogany pail, the other a chamber pot – before plumbed-in toilets, chamber-pots were available for the relief of diners, even in the grandest houses, to be used behind a folding screen.

Keeping smells at bay

There is a comparative absence of soft furnishings; writing in 1772, Adam insisted that his eating rooms should be 'always finished with stucco, and adorned with statues and paintings, that they may not retain the smell of the victuals'. For the same reason, the kitchen at Osterley was located on the floor below, and was later moved to the other side of the house. Convoys of servants would hurry with hot dishes up a staircase, emerging through a discreet door in a corner of the Eating Room, to the right of the fireplace.

The dishes were brought in by footmen and placed in the centre of the table. Guests helped one another to food, and the footmen would assist by taking plates to the host who was wielding the ladle or tongs.

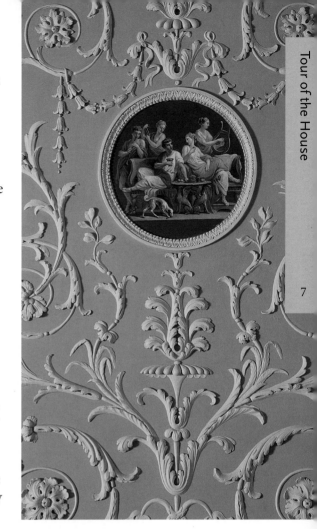

Feasts for the eye

Dining in impressive style was a feature of 18th-century life, and dinner was usually served around 4 or 5pm. A great deal of effort, time and money was expended by the fashionable in the pursuit of the edible, and the Child family were no exception. Menus were intricate and had to be a feast for the eyes as well as the stomach. At Osterley, dinner might include venison from the estate, or pigeons from the dovecote. Vegetables would accompany main dishes, but only in small quantities – they were looked down on as being lower-class. Exotic spices were much in vogue, and cosmopolitan, wealthy families experimented with the dishes newly available through the trade with Asia. The enduring British passion for curry began with 18th-century menus.

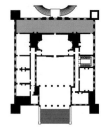

THE LONG GALLERY

The room is approximately 40 metres long (130 feet), and occupies the whole length of the garden front. A Long Gallery was a traditional feature of Tudor houses, and examples survive at other National Trust properties, such as Montacute and Hardwick Hall. They were intended as a place for exercise in poor weather, for the playing of games, even dancing. As such, they usually contained little furniture, but their dimensions and function made them ideal for the display of tapestries or paintings.

Below The gilt girandoles were designed by Adam specially for this room

A place for pictures

In 1756–9 Matthew Hillyard was charged with creating a gallery to house the family's large collection of pictures. He reused old joinery, taking his inspiration from Inigo Jones's design for Charles I's chapel at Somerset House. Hillyard also designed a frieze featuring stylised marigolds, the flower used as the logo of Child's Bank. The 1782 inventory states that among the 49 paintings in this room were works by Van Dyck, Murillo, Claude Lorraine, Poussin, Lely, Rubens and Titian. (Sadly, most of them were lost in a fire on Jersey in 1949.) The paintings on display here today are mostly on loan from the Victoria & Albert Museum and the Royal Collection. They evoke the type of pictures that would have hung here in the 1780s. (A detailed list is available in the room.)

The Neo-classical architect William Chambers (1723–96) designed the marble *chimneypieces*, and after 1764 Robert Adam filled in the Venetian windows at either end of the room and hung pea-green wallpaper. He also designed spectacular pier-glasses (mirrors) for this room; the six large *girandoles* (candelabras) with unusual heart-shaped frames were probably made by John Linnell, as was the furniture.

Above Gaspard Dughet's *Classical Landscape* is typical of the kind of Old Master paintings that would have hung in the Long Gallery in the 18th century

Oriental obsessions

Robert Child's uncle, father and grandfather were directors of the East India Company, which imported tea, coffee, spices, cotton, silk, chintz and ceramics from India and China. This rich and powerful organisation had been set up in 1600 to allow enterprising English traders to secure supplies of spices and exotic goods in competition with the Portuguese and the Dutch. It operated for more than 250 years, and was highly influential in successfully expanding Britain's trading networks and, eventually, her Imperial ambitions.

Osterley was built from the profits of lucrative international trade. Oriental objects were highly fashionable at this time, and this room reflects the passion for *chinoiserie* sweeping Europe. The ***pagodas*** and the two pairs of Chinese *famille rose* mandarin ***jars*** date from the 18th century, as do the virtuoso pair of ***imperial junks carved from elephant ivory*** (illustrated); the dragon-headed junk represented the Chinese Emperor, and its phoenix-headed counterpart the Empress.

THE DRAWING ROOM

After formal dinners, the 18th-century society hostess would 'withdraw' by leading the other ladies to her 'drawing room', leaving the gentlemen to drink liqueurs, smoke and talk politics or business in the Eating Room. At Osterley, the Entrance Hall separates the Eating Room from the Drawing Room, an arrangement that ensured that neither group could overhear any indiscretion from the other. The ladies would drink tea, chocolate or coffee together until the men came to join them. On less formal occasions, when the household had no guests, the entire family would relax in the Drawing Room immediately after dinner and play cards, sing or play a musical instrument. The hostess would preside over the making of the tea, using the very best quality leaves and the most impressive china.

The faded silk damask seen on the walls today was installed in the late 19th century; Adam's scheme, dating from the mid-1760s, was originally a pale green colour. The *frieze* of scrolled foliage is in gold on a dark crimson background. The gold-coloured **grate and fender** are made of paktong, an alloy of copper, nickel and zinc.

Below Adam's design for the Drawing Room grate

Furniture
The eight carved and gilt **armchairs** and two **sofas** with Rococo shell ornaments and cabriole legs were designed and made for this room by John Linnell in 1769. The pair of bow-fronted **commodes** was designed by Adam in 1773; veneered with hardwood, satinwood and other woods, and mounted with ormolu (gilt bronze). The Neo-classical **roundels** were inspired by paintings by Angelica Kauffman, the most successful female artist of the 18th century. The commodes were purely decorative, designed to complement the impressive **pier-glasses**, which, at 251 by 132cm (8 feet 3 inches by 4 feet 4 inches), were too large for British manufacturers and had to be made to order in France. The two **tripods** are Adam-style candlestands of carved and gilt wood, decorated with stylised rams' heads which relate to those under the brackets of the chimneypiece and the door architraves.

Ornamenting the mantelpiece
The mantelpiece supports two pairs of magnificent ormolu-mounted (gilt bronze) spar **vases**, made by Matthew Boulton (1728–1809). Robert Child collected these decorative pieces because he admired the workmanship involved in carving and polishing a single piece of bluejohn (a subtly coloured stone mined in the Peak District in Derbyshire), and its intricate mounting in metal. A further piece from his collection may be seen in the Breakfast Room.

Left
The Drawing
Room

Sunburst ceiling

The ceiling is based on an engraving of
the antique Temple of the Sun,
published by Robert Wood in his book
Ruins of Palmyra in 1753; Palmyra is in
present-day Syria. Adam may also have
been influenced by a *trompe-l'oeil*
(illusionistic) ceiling in the nave of
West Wycombe church, painted for
Lord Dashwood by Giuseppe Mattia
Borgnis (1701–61), whose son was later
to paint the Etruscan Dressing Room
at Osterley. In order to make the
Palmyra design fit the rectangular
Drawing Room, Adam 'stretched' the
central circular motif into an oval, and
designed a carpet to match.

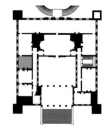

THE TAPESTRY ROOM

This is the first of the three rooms that make up the State Apartment, a suite created to impress and entertain very important guests, such as royalty. By the late 18th century, such suites had fallen out of fashion. As in other rooms at Osterley, Adam designed the ceiling first; the central medallion depicts *The dedication of a child to Minerva*.

Tapestries

The magnificent set of tapestries was woven by hand on vertical looms, and took four years to complete. It was ordered from the Gobelins factory in Paris in 1772; records reveal a set executed in 1775–6 'pour un seigneur anglais' and delivered to Osterley in July 1776.

Right
The Tapestry Room

'The most superb and beautiful [room] that can be imagined.'

Horace Walpole

This kind of decoration is known as medallion tapestry, because the design features medallion-like cartouches of gold-framed figurative images, set against a background woven to look like crimson damask. The medallion images were designed by the painter François Boucher (1703–70). They represent the Four Elements, fire, earth, air and water, as personified by the Loves of the Gods, with the pier-glass representing water. The characters featured include *Cupid and Psyche* over the chimneypiece; *Venus and Vulcan* (fire) opposite; *Aurora and Cephalus* (air) and *Vertumnus and Pomona* (earth) face the windows. The strong architectural mood is softened by swags and garlands of fruit and flowers. There are subtle references to Mrs Child's love of her garden and her menagerie in the imagery of animals and birds, including a rabbit, badger and porcupine – even Sarah's gardening hat is depicted.

The integration of the tapestries with every other feature of this room is remarkable; Adam designed a pier-table with three painted plaques which echo the inlaid scagliola (imitation marble) cameos on the chimneypiece. The pier-glass frame was designed to complement the tapestries; the pedestal and bowl of flowers are flanked by two standing females holding garlands which appear to emerge from the tapestry.

After the tapestries had been installed, Adam added a pair of tripod **pedestals** to support a brace of ormolu candlestands. He also designed a **carpet**, made by Thomas Moore (active 1756–78), which incorporates large baskets of flowers to co-ordinate with the flower vases depicted on the walls.

Upholstered to match

The sofa and eight **armchairs** are upholstered in matching tapestry, with Boucher's *Jeux d'Enfants* in oval frames on the backs. These designs had been made exclusively for the French king's mistress, Madame de Pompadour, in 1751–3, and their reproduction for other clients was only authorised after her death in 1770.

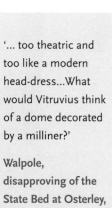

THE STATE BEDCHAMBER

Adam's extraordinary *Design of a Bed for Robert Child Esqr* has survived in the Soane Museum. More surprisingly, the State Bed still dominates the room for which it was intended at Osterley. Magnificent and opulent, this domed, lacquered and festooned eight-poster is a strange blend of a classical temple and a theatrical stage setting. It is significant that at the same time that Adam was designing this bed, he was also creating a lavishly canopied box for King George III at the Italian Theatre in the Haymarket.

Designed to impress

The State Bed is 4.45 metres high (14 feet 5 inches) and 2.28 metres (7 feet 5 inches) wide, and a set of steps was required to gain access to it. The room was intended to impress rather than for daily use; Robert and Sarah Child actually slept in a much more modest room on the floor above. Once again, the very large and expensive pier-glasses were imported from France as British makers could not produce anything so ambitious. Apparently, the decoration and installation of this room and its contents were so expensive that Robert Child ripped up the bill after paying it so that no one would know how much he had spent.

Adam also provided designs for the embroidered bedhangings and counterpane, as well as the interior of the dome, which can be seen with the aid of a mirror. Much attention was paid to the decoration, which features nymphs, garlands, flowers and dolphins. Marigolds (symbolising Child's Bank) appear on the valance, as well as the Child family crest of an eagle holding an adder in its beak. The poppy heads on the curtain cornices symbolise sleep.

'... too theatric and too like a modern head-dress...What would Vitruvius think of a dome decorated by a milliner?'

Walpole, disapproving of the State Bed at Osterley, in a letter, 1778

Dedicated to love

The State Bedchamber was decorated with subtle references to romance and fertility. The *ceiling* has a painted central medallion inspired by Angelica Kauffman's painting of Aglaia, one of the Three Graces, being enslaved by Love. The smaller ceiling paintings around the central medallion have been attributed to Zucchi, and feature pastoral scenes.

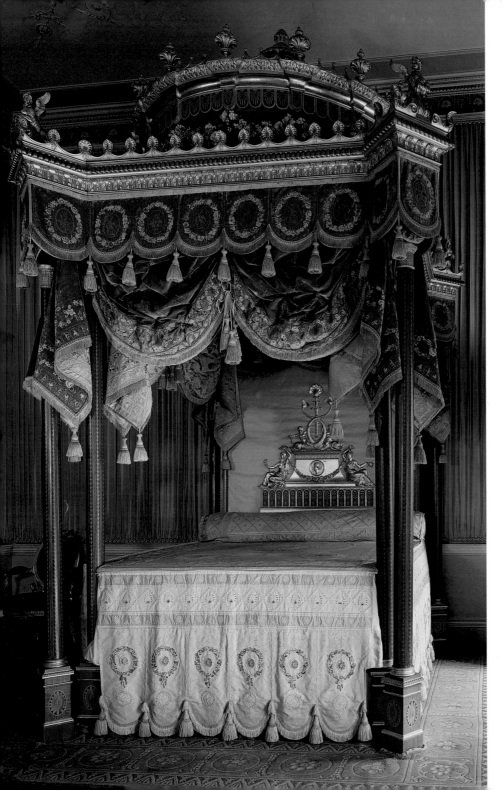

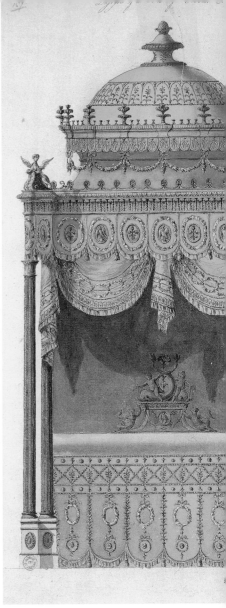

Above Adam's design for the State Bed

Left The State Bedchamber

THE ETRUSCAN DRESSING ROOM

The Etruscan Dressing Room was the third element of Adam's State Apartment, and it was intended to be a sitting room or ante-chamber to the State Bedchamber. Although State Apartments were falling out of use by the late 18th century, Adam's design for this room was avant-garde by the standards of its day, taking inspiration from a variety of antique sources to create a harmonious setting. Adam designed almost everything in this room, from the pier-glass to a set of eight armchairs – even the embroidered panel on the tripod fire-screen was stitched by Mrs Child to his design. His scheme for the decoration of the walls was inspired by recent archaeological discoveries in Etruria in central Italy.

Right The Etruscan Dressing Room

Below The ceiling of the Etruscan Dressing Room

Antique inspiration

Adam was intrigued by the antique Etruscan vases in Sir William Hamilton's collection, illustrations of which had recently been published, but he admitted frankly that there was no evidence that such colour schemes or decorative style had ever been applied to interior design in classical times. However, he would have been familiar with the 'Etruscan'-style ceramic tablets and medallions being manufactured by Josiah Wedgwood (1730–95) as early as 1769. Wedgwood's advertisements described his wares as '… black basalts with Etruscan red burnt-in grounds…for inlaying in the panels of rooms…hanging up as ornaments in libraries…or as Pictures for Dressing Rooms….'

Adam's designs for the walls of the Etruscan Dressing Room were completed in 1775 and copied by the ornament painter Pietro Maria Borgnis (1739/43–1810) on sheets of paper, which were then pasted onto canvas and fixed to the walls and ceiling using battens. A soft

sky blue is the ground colour of the walls, a contrast to the grandeur and opulence of the State Bedchamber next door. The room has an airy, light, almost out-of-doors feel – Walpole saw the Dressing Room as a sort of pergola, '… a pretty waiting room in a garden…'

Furniture

Even the furniture has a lightness of touch: the black and gold border of the *pier-glass* harmonises with the *commode* (which incorporates panels of oriental lacquer), probably supplied by Chippendale. A black and gold japanned *Pembroke table* blends Neo-classicism with *Chinoiserie*. The subject is taken from one of Sir William Hamilton's classical vases, but the materials imitate the effect of luxurious imports from the Far East.

THE SOUTH CORRIDOR AND VESTIBULE

The South Corridor contains Chinese black and gold lacquered *chairs* bearing the Child arms. The set was made in the 1720s for Sir Francis Child the Younger, a director of the East India Company, and was probably ordered at the same time as the very unusual Chinese porcelain service to be seen in Mr Child's Dressing Room. Export wares for 18th-century western clients tended to be made or sourced in Canton (present-day Guangzhou), where the East India Company maintained an important trading base. The impressive eight-panelled *black lacquer screen* is typical of export wares from south China, and also dates from the same era. The furniture was intended for the family house in Lincoln's Inn Fields; when this was sold in 1767, several pieces were

From sitting room to school room

The 9th Earl of Jersey remembered this room being used as his school room in the early 20th century. Visitors today will be surprised to see a dark square on the wall above the left-hand window; this reveals how polluted and smoke-blackened the room had become before it was conserved.

Below Old lacquer is fragile and needs to be handled carefully with gloves

17

sent to Osterley. The corridor leads into the South Vestibule, which contains a display of the family's magnificent *porcelain*, including some important 18th-century Sèvres pieces.

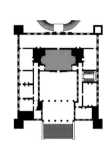

THE ENTRANCE HALL

Adam's Entrance Hall replaced the earlier hall on the east side of the building, which was demolished when the portico was created. Visitors were required to climb the steps, walk between the impressive columns, advance across the courtyard and enter the Hall. Rooms like this were often used for large dinners, parties and balls, and were intended to impress.

Above The alcoves give variety to the room

'... the glory that was Greece, and the grandeur that was Rome....'

Edgar Allan Poe, 'To Helen',1831

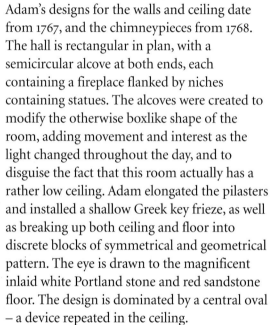

Adam's designs for the walls and ceiling date from 1767, and the chimneypieces from 1768. The hall is rectangular in plan, with a semicircular alcove at both ends, each containing a fireplace flanked by niches containing statues. The alcoves were created to modify the otherwise boxlike shape of the room, adding movement and interest as the light changed throughout the day, and to disguise the fact that this room actually has a rather low ceiling. Adam elongated the pilasters and installed a shallow Greek key frieze, as well as breaking up both ceiling and floor into discrete blocks of symmetrical and geometrical pattern. The eye is drawn to the magnificent inlaid white Portland stone and red sandstone floor. The design is dominated by a central oval – a device repeated in the ceiling.

There is a martial theme to the stuccowork panels, showing assemblages of arms and armour. Here Adam was subtly referring to the medieval custom of storing weapons in large houses. The panels were inspired by the trophies of arms in the Emperor Augustus's palace on the Campidoglio in Rome, a classical site with which Adam was familiar.

The Portland stone fireplaces incorporate the Child family crest of an eagle holding an adder in its beak. Above each is a *grisaille*

(monochrome) painted panel; in convincing *trompe-l'oeil*, they imitate low-relief carvings. Both panels were executed by Cipriani; one represents *The Triumph of Ceres*, the goddess of plenty, and the other *The Triumph of Bacchus*, the god of wine. The coffered ceilings of each alcove are a reference to the Basilica of Maxentius in Rome. In the niches are 18th-century copies of antique statues of Hercules, Ceres, Apollo and Minerva. Flanking the alcoves are four marble vases with relief figures on carved and painted pedestals, possibly by William Chambers.

The original colour scheme was white and three shades of French grey, a limited palette of great subtlety. The three-branched oil lamps and the four 'scroll end stools' were designed by Adam – another example of his commitment to total design.

The classical world re-interpreted

This scheme is a consummate example of the architect's skill in re-interpreting the essence of the classical world for his wealthy and sophisticated clients and their contemporaries. The imagery and motifs Adam used are a blend of influences from ancient Greece and Rome (though Roman themes predominate here). The design of the frieze and the pilasters (square-

fronted columns) were inspired by Adam's detailed studies of the ruins of the Palace of the Emperor Diocletian at Split, in present-day Croatia. Other Roman motifs include vases, urns, scrolls and sphinxes, linked with painted swags and ribbons. The Neo-classical decoration – from the stone colour scheme to the romantic landscape outside, framed by the pillars of the portico – reflected prevailing cultural aspirations. It also provided an imaginative solution to the practical problem of reworking an existing building.

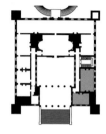

THE LIBRARY

The Library was commissioned by Francis Child to house his magnificent book collection. Unfortunately, the collection had to be sold in 1885 in order to renew the roof. Very few of the books here today are indigenous, but they represent the type of works typically found in a gentleman's library of the time. Although there were books here belonging to Sarah Child, the room was primarily a masculine retreat and a place where Robert Child could read, write or conduct his business affairs undisturbed by the rest of the household.

Decoration

The emphasis of the decorative scheme is overtly architectural and rectilinear; Ionic frontispieces grace the centre of each of the sets of bookshelves facing the windows, and Ionic pilasters frame the subsidiary shelves. The ceiling was one of three alternative designs Adam prepared for this room; a similar monochromatic scheme was used in the hall at Syon nearby.

decorated with Vitruvian (wave-like) scrolls in marquetry. The eight lyre-backed *armchairs* each bear an ormolu cameo of a classical head. The large pedestal *desk* is embellished with symbols of architecture, sculpture, painting and music, inlaid in subtly different woods with great skill.

Right One of the Library chimneypieces

Furniture

The ormolu-mounted furniture is a spectacular suite in the French Neo-classical style, known as *goût grec*, or Grecian style, and was supplied by John Linnell. Each piece is

Pictures

The pictures are all by Antonio Zucchi and have a common theme, the Arts and Sciences, appropriate for a library. Zucchi had been persuaded by James Adam to leave his native Italy and work with the brothers in England. He remained Robert Adam's principal decorative painter until 1781, when he married the painter Angelica Kauffman.

THE BREAKFAST ROOM

In this room the Child family would eat breakfast, and sometimes other meals were served here when they had no guests or visitors. It was also used as an informal sitting room during the day, as it has an excellent view of the park with its woods and lakes and receives the morning sunshine. Pastimes might include painting, harpsichord-playing and music lessons - all part of the repertoire of 'accomplishments' expected of gentlewomen.

Pictures
The walls were bright yellow in the late 18th century, and covered in paintings; the 1782 inventory lists 41 paintings in this room alone, including works by Claude Lorraine, Nicolas Poussin and Canaletto, and a portrait of Miss Child by Sir Joshua Reynolds. Unfortunately, these pictures, like those formerly in the Long Gallery, were removed from the house when it was given to the National Trust.

Furniture
The furniture here is mostly by John Linnell and it is thought that Adam's only contribution to the decoration is the pair of arched pier-glasses and pier-tables – his design for these is dated 1777.

Making music

Robert Child's only daughter, Sarah Anne (1764-93), was the favourite pupil of Gabriel Piozzi, who composed music especially for her. The harpsichord was made for her in 1781 by the celebrated English maker Jacob Kirkman and his nephew Abraham. When Sarah Anne died in 1793, this harpsichord was sent to her grieving husband at his request, so it must have meant a great deal to her. It was returned to Osterley by their daughter, Lady Jersey, when she refurbished the house in 1805.

THE GREAT STAIR

This imposing staircase rises from what was the family entrance on the ground floor to the bedrooms on the second floor. The principal floor is distinguished by the use of Corinthian columns, the floor above sporting Ionic columns. The wrought-iron balusters are decorated with classical anthemions (honeysuckle) and are identical to those Adam designed for Kenwood, which are known to date from 1769. On the walls, friezes and panels of stucco depict vases and ewers, symbols of hospitality. The mahogany banister rail is carved with Vitruvian scrolls to match the wall moulding, typical of Adam's attention to detail.

Ceiling painting

Adam's original design for the staircase was modified in 1768 to accommodate a magnificent 17th-century ceiling painting by Rubens, *The Glorification of the Duke of Buckingham*. The version you see today is a copy made from original sketches, as the original painting was among those removed from the house and destroyed by fire in 1949.

Lighting

On the principal floor, the Great Stair was lit by pendant *oil lamps* in the antique style, described in the 1782 inventory as 'Three elegant Lamps mounted in Or Molee [ormolu] with brass ballance weights lines Tassells and double pullies….' In addition, on the half-landing there is a pair of *lanterns* placed on carved and painted wood tripod pedestals with rams' heads.

Left The Great Stair

THE YELLOW TAFFETA BEDCHAMBER

Initially remodelled in 1759, this was the principal guest bedroom. To modern eyes it may seem sparsely furnished, but that was standard 18th-century practice. In families with any pretensions to gentility, each bedroom would have its own dressing room, and it was here that you would bathe, dress and store your clothes. Therefore a bedroom remained largely that – predominantly a room with a bed in it. The 'Taffety Dressing Room' (which was adjacent to the Yellow Taffeta Bedchamber and was reached by a concealed door to the right of the bed) unfortunately no longer exists, but records show that it had curtains of the same painted satin Deccan work, imported from southern India, and four armchairs identical to those in the bedroom.

Furniture

The matching suite of satinwood furniture was designed by John Linnell. The small 'toilet' *table* has a skirt of fine Indian muslin, a 20th-century replica of the original fabric. Jugs of hot water would be brought every morning by the maid so that the room's occupants could wash, and a chamber-pot would be placed discreetly in each night table. Houses in the 18th century had no running water, so the occupants relied on servants to supply and remove fresh water and chamber-pots.

The gilt frames for the *pier-glass* and the Chinese *overmantel picture* painted on glass have honeysuckle motifs and scrolled foliage to match the frieze on the chimneypiece, which was probably from a design by William Chambers.

Top right The dressing table in the Yellow Taffeta Bedchamber is covered in Indian muslin

Bed

The four-poster bed was designed by Robert Adam in 1779, his last design for furniture at Osterley. It has a concave cornice of satinwood veneer, inlaid with green-stained wood; carved and gilded putti and stylised honeysuckle complete the decoration of the frame. The pale yellow silk taffeta curtains around the bed and at the window were made in the 1920s in imitation of the 18th-century originals.

MR CHILD'S DRESSING ROOM

Robert and Sarah Child's private apartments started at the left of the head of the Great Stair, with Mr Child's Dressing Room and Bedroom, interconnecting rooms which were refurbished for Francis Child in 1759. Old materials were re-used whenever possible – the door surrounds, for example, date from the late 17th century.

The suite of furniture made for Mr Child's Dressing Room is no longer at Osterley; records show that he had blue silk curtains and a blue Brussels carpet, an oval pier-glass in a carved and painted frame, a mahogany wardrobe, a shaving stand and a commode. This room now tells the story of the Child family.

Ceramics

Right Meissen dinner plate

In the glass-fronted cabinets are some fascinating export ware ceramics, part of a *dinner service* bearing the arms of the Child family, probably made in China in the 1720s for Francis Child, who was a director of the East India Company at the time. It is the only one known in existence to have a powder-blue border. In the 1820s the Jerseys commissioned further pieces to match, such as ice-pails and entrée dishes. Also on display are plates from the Jersey *Meissen dinner service*.

MR CHILD'S BEDCHAMBER

This room was shared by Robert and Sarah Child when they were in residence at Osterley, mostly between May and November.

They were married in 1763, as a newspaper of the time announced:

This day Robert Child. Esq., the only Brother and heir to the great estate and fortune of Francis Child, Esq....was married at Wraybury, in the county of Bucks, to Miss Jodrell, eldest Daughter of Gilbert Jodrell of Ankerwyke, Esq. A young Lady of distinguished Beauty, merit, and a Fortune of £10,000.

Bed

Designed for Robert's brother Francis, who died shortly before he was due to marry, the mahogany four-poster bed was originally hung with Indian embroidered silks, but only the valances and bed cornices have survived. There is a set of *steps* by the bed, which was supplied for the State Bed downstairs in the 1880s.

The intricately decorated *ebony cabinet* to the right of the fireplace is French, and its interior is embellished with tortoiseshell, ivory and rosewood marquetry.

'...full of pictures, gold filigree, china and japan....'

Horace Walpole, describing Mrs Child's Dressing Room

MRS CHILD'S DRESSING ROOM

Sarah Child dressed and stored her clothes in this room, which also served as a boudoir, an informal and comfortable room where she could relax.

She entertained female houseguests here, while the gentlemen were out hunting. Their time would be spent in conversation, playing cards, embroidering and drinking tea and coffee. Interestingly, the 1782 inventory also details 'A Pocket Telescope' as being in this room, so Mrs Child's day-to-day activities were probably not as introverted as might have been assumed; from the window in the corridor outside, one can see into the stableyard and her pride and joy – the garden.

Above Indian embroidered silks decorate the four-poster bed in Mr Child's Bedroom

Left Mrs Child's Dressing Room. The carved wooden *chimneypiece* was designed and made by John Linnell. The gilt overmantel incorporates brackets for displaying fine porcelain, and a portrait of Sarah Anne Child at about four years old, which was executed by Francis Cotes in crayon. Sarah Anne had a suite of rooms in the south wing

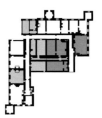

THE GROUND FLOOR

In the 18th century the ground floor was a complex of well-organised apartments with an efficient staff, all geared to making 'above stairs' life appear orderly and serene. The Kitchen was originally located at the opposite corner of the house and was moved here in the 19th century.

THE STRONG ROOM

Silver

In 1929–31 the Strong Room was fitted out with cabinets to house the magnificent collection of family silver, which dates back as far as the 1690s. When the family were in residence in the 18th century, gold and silver vessels and plates would have been displayed on the sideboard in the Eating Room for special occasions. The Strong Room cases are full of the Child and Jersey families' collections of gold and silver plate, coins, medals and weaponry, as well as a magnificent silver wine cistern.

THE SERVANTS' HALL

The Servants' Hall has a black and white stone-flagged floor, and a vaulted ceiling. The majority of the household staff ate all their meals in this room; it was basic but comfortable, with a substantial fireplace, and in the 18th century would have been fitted with two long deal wooden tables, seven forms and ten wooden-bottomed chairs. The 1782 inventory records 'A Glass in a black frame' here – presumably a mirror, to encourage servants to take a pride in their appearances.

THE WINE AND BEER CELLARS

Traces of the brickwork of the original Tudor building can be seen at this level, in particular the passage wall near the cellar. The extensive wine and beer cellars run under the Entrance Hall, an arrangement that kept the temperature constant. In the 18th century, beer was commonly drunk instead of water, as it was known to be more hygienic. At Osterley, beer was made in the brewhouse in the stableyard and then piped down to the cellar where it was available on tap. The weakest variety was known as 'small beer', and was

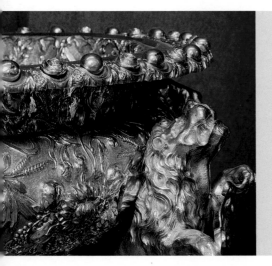

The huge **silver cistern** (wine cooler) weighs 1,680 ounces. It is hallmarked for 1695 and is the second largest cistern to survive from the 17th century.

Engraved with the royal coat of arms, it may originally have been used by an ambassador serving in an important foreign posting.

given to servants and children. The strongest and most potent brew was reserved for members of the family and their guests.

Wine was also stored here, in large wooden casks. Each day the butler would decant quantities of the wine stored in the cellar and prepare it by either standing it in his pantry to reach room temperature if it was red, or packing it in ice brought in from the ice-house if it was white.

The supply and storage of wine and beer was the duty of the butler, and he also maintained the inventory or cellar book, so to manage stock rotation without endangering supplies of his master's favourite tipple.

Above
The Servants' Hall

THE SERVANTS

SUMMONING HELP

The Childs introduced an innovation which streamlined domestic life. They abandoned the long-standing practice of having servants in attendance outside every room, and installed a system of bells to summon specific staff from their hall downstairs when required, one of the first such systems in this country.

An army of staff

In the 18th century, when the family was in residence, there were some 28 household servants and about 20 gardeners. Those figures were seasonal – during the winter, when fashionable families stayed in London and the Childs were at their other house in Berkeley Square, only a skeleton staff stayed on at Osterley to maintain the house.

Servants' livery

The male servants were provided with livery, tailored to fit, at the rate of one suit a year.

Their smart appearance was a status symbol, reflecting on their employer. A typical outfit for a footman consisted of a frock coat, a waistcoat, breeches, a shirt and stock, and stockings. Female servants were less highly valued and so less well rewarded; they usually provided their own clothes, as their role was to work 'behind the scenes'. However, they did receive 'bed and board', which provided security and independence in an era when the only route to prosperity available to a girl of humble origins was a fortunate marriage.

Getting on

For all classes of servants there were opportunities for advancement. The scullery-maid might be promoted to the role of kitchen-maid; a bright kitchenmaid could be trained up to assist the cook, and eventually run her own kitchen. The hall-boy might eventually become an under-footman, and a footman might make it to butler, the senior servant, responsible for running the dining room staff, the footmen, the wine cellar and the Strong Room. Status was also important; the laundrymaid earned more than the housemaid, but being a housemaid was considered 'refined'.

Female staff in 1787–8

Rachael Holmes	*Housekeeper*	Jane Collins	*Stillroom maid*
Mary Kitchman	*Lady's maid*	Elizabeth Huggins	*Dairymaid*
Ann Ellis	*Chambermaid*	Sarah Protton	*Kitchenmaid*
Martha Bishop	*Cook*	Frances Woodroffe	*Kitchenmaid*
Ann Malius	*Upper Housemaid*	Frances Buckell	*Laundrymaid*
Elizabeth Smith	*2nd Housemaid*	Elizabeth Rudditt	*Poultry woman*
Elizabeth England	*3rd Housemaid*		

THE STEWARD'S AND MRS BUNCE'S ROOMS

These two rooms were used by the senior staff, who liaised between the Child family and the rest of the domestic household. In the late 18th century, the Steward at Osterley, Edward Bunce, was assisted by his wife in an administrative capacity.

Mrs Bunce's room was furnished in the 1780s as a comfortable office with armchairs, a carpet, a bookshelf and a painting of a seascape. The dark wooden panelling, concealing cupboards that feature wig stands and a safe, was installed in the 19th century.

In the 18th century some of the more senior servants staying at the house with their masters and mistresses would eat in the Steward's Room with Mr Bunce, an indication of their higher status. He ran many aspects of the considerable estate for Mr Child. There were the three houses, Osterley, Berkeley Square and Upton, and Mr Bunce handled all the accounts, expenditure, building work and servants' discipline.

Below The Steward's Room is shown as it was left in the 1970s by the 9th Earl of Jersey

THE KITCHEN

The Kitchen was the hub of domestic operations, a hive of activity, and undoubtedly a hot and noisy working environment. The worn-down stone steps at the entrance testify to the incessant comings and goings; food was constantly being delivered, prepared, plated up and taken at speed to its destination, and the staff were marshalled and chivvied by the cook. In Robert and Sarah's time, Mrs Martha Bishop ran the Kitchen; cooks were always known as 'Mrs' as a courtesy title, regardless of their marital status. She was assisted by two kitchen-maids, and the family's footmen slept in a bedroom next to the Kitchen.

In the 18th century, all food was cooked over a huge open fire or on a **cooking range** – the one now *in situ* was installed in the 1920s, and there was another range (now removed),

which was located beneath the windows. The **bread oven** dates from the 18th century, and the **pastry oven** from around 1850. The ovens were fed with coal stored in the coal pens on the same floor. The extent of these stores with their waist-high barriers is an indication of the massive fuel consumption of Osterley. The coal was brought into the house via doors at the side of the front steps.

The Kitchen shelves would have been full of pewter plates and a copper *batterie de cuisine*, ranging from saucepans of every imaginable size to 91 intricate moulds for jellies and blancmanges. The vast **table top** was made from a single trunk; servants worked on either side of this surface preparing food. The large **wooden rack** was used to carry ice from the ice-house in the grounds, or for bringing in large sides of meat.

THE SCULLERY

The small Scullery off the Kitchen has a double sink, fitted with a wooden surround to help protect the delicate glass and china as they were being washed. Although now fitted with taps, in the 18th century there was no running water, so all water would have to be brought into the Kitchen area and heated on the fire before use. Every item used had to be washed by hand, so a scullery maid's existence was not an enviable one.

THE PASTRY ROOM

The Pastry Room needed to maintain a low temperature; the marble slab and the stable-door allowed this room to stay cool while pies and pastries were being prepared.

Right The Scullery sinks are lined with lead

Food preparation

Money was no object when it came to the most luxurious provisions; some typical entries from the late 18th-century account books include:

One week's supply of fish, including sole, shrimps, lobster, prawns, and turbot - £9 2s 9d.

Bill from Wilson, Thornhill and Wilson of 77 St Paul's Churchyard for a year's supply of coffee, tea, chocolate and sugar for Berkeley Square and Osterley - £225 2s 4d.

This was at a time when a kitchenmaid would earn £7 a year. Much of the food consumed at Osterley was grown on the estate, such as venison, lamb, mutton, dairy produce and even honey, as well as vegetables and fruit. But basic provisions like flour or sugar would be bought in from local tradespeople, and luxuries such as drinking chocolate and exotic spices were frequently transported the eight miles from central London to supply the family and their guests. All fresh produce had to be delivered and consumed promptly, as there was no refrigeration.

THE GARDEN

The garden and grounds of Osterley Park have survived to the present day largely unaltered from the state of elegance they attained in the late 18th century. The essence of the small country estate is still visible, largely due to benign lack of interest in radical renovation on the part of successive Earls of Jersey, who owned the estate throughout the 19th and the first half of the 20th centuries.

Right Osterley Park in the mid-18th century

Opposite The view from the portico across the park

It is not known who designed the grounds for Francis and Robert Child, but Robert Adam may well have been involved, as there are similarities with the layout at nearby Syon Park, and Kedleston Hall in Derbyshire where he was also employed. Certainly, vistas and carefully contrived viewpoints hint at Adam's controlling genius: for example, the semicircular Garden House stands five metres away from a Tudor wall, but when viewed from Mrs Child's Dressing Room (the room she used as a boudoir), the Garden House appears to be growing out of the wall. There was also a completely clear view down to the Temple of Pan from the Dressing Room window in Mrs Child's day.

The 145-hectare (357-acre) park has lime-free soil, with gravel in some areas and clay in others. It lies at 30 metres (100 feet) above sea-level and is predominantly flat. For this reason it was criticised by some 18th-century visitors for being featureless, though fertile. Robert and Sarah Child introduced magnificent trees and plants, to create an idealised landscape. The park is especially attractive in spring months, with drifts of bluebells carpeting the woods. The many fine trees include oaks such as *Quercus cerris*, *Quercus frainetto*, Daimyo, Turkey and Hungary oaks.

There is still a thriving home farm, though this is now tenanted. What was a substantial walled garden providing food for the estate in the 18th century is also leased out and worked as a market garden.

RESTORING THE GARDEN

Staff and volunteers at Osterley are fortunate in that the inventory of 1782, compiled on the death of Robert Child, lists the plants, trees, captive animals and birds in the gardens and grounds. It is therefore comparatively easy to identify what was grown here, and to reinstate it where possible. The Trust has embarked upon a major programme of restoration of the grounds and gardens at Osterley in recent years. The great storms of 1987 and 1990 brought down more than 200 mature trees, which necessitated extensive clearance and replanting. More recently, gardeners and volunteers cleared great stretches of the Long Walk of scrub and undergrowth.

The American Garden is being re-instated, and plans are underway to move the estate fencing back to where it was in the 18th century. In addition, thickets of laurel have been cleared from part of the Great Meadow so as to return it to its former appearance.

1 MRS CHILD'S FLOWER GARDEN

Numbers in this section refer to the bird's-eye view and key inside the front cover.

Mrs Sarah Child lived at Osterley from 1763 until her death in 1793. She was a keen gardener and was instrumental in creating the garden that bears her name. She purchased the most fashionable and exotic plants available at that time. The Flower Garden was designed to be at its best in the summer months, when the family spent most time at Osterley. Mrs Child's Flower Garden features a series of flowerbeds and paths which radiate out from the Garden House. The beds are planted according to a 1780s plant list and feature vibrantly coloured flowers all summer long.

Below The Garden House

The cultivation of flowers was considered a suitable pastime for gentlewomen in the 18th century, and Mrs Child also used the flower garden as inspiration for her embroidery – many examples of her needlework portray flowers known to have grown in her garden, while her discarded gardening hat is portrayed on one of the magnificent textiles in the Tapestry Room.

2 THE GARDEN HOUSE

The semicircular Garden House is decorated with stucco medallions of festive figures and Ionic pilasters. It was built in 1780, and is in near-original condition, although it did once have sphinxes at the end of each parapet, which have now disappeared. It was designed by Adam as a greenhouse and is still used for displaying tender plants such as orange and lemon trees. The temperature rarely drops below three degrees centigrade in the Garden House, so sensitive and even tropical plants could be nurtured through the darkest and coldest months, then brought out while family was in residence. The 1782 inventory details 'Forty five Orange and Lemon trees in tubs and Twelve circular Stands for ditto'. The Garden House and the nearby Orangery (now lost) were also used for growing prestigious rarities such as grapes, pineapples and mimosa.

Opposite, top Mrs Child's Flower Garden **Bottom** The interior of the Garden House

3 THE AMERICAN GARDEN

The American Garden is being reinstated thanks to financial support from Royal Oak, the National Trust's American affiliate. In the 18th century, wealthy and fashionable Europeans were fascinated by plants and trees from the New World, and as a status symbol some created special gardens in which to grow rare specimens from the Americas. Very few have survived, as the Victorian fashion for rhododendrons tended to overpower these specimen gardens; there is an example at Painshill in Surrey, in a rather formal walled enclosure.

Below The Orangery was burned down during the Second World War

The American Garden is being restored in the form of a woodland border and being replanted with the same trees, shrubs, herbaceous woodlanders, bulbs and roses listed as being here in 1785. Many of these are still rare in Britain; specimens include Liquidambar and *Calicanthus*. They have been planted quite wide apart in 'specimen style', as each plant was meant to be viewed in isolation, rather than creating an overall impression, as in herbaceous borders

today. Research has shown that the American Garden was designed to provide a variety of microclimates, allowing the gardeners to experiment with differing growing conditions for these exotic and unfamiliar plants. The space was divided by low hedges, and seeds of the same species would have been planted in varying aspects (shady, north-facing, in full sun, south-facing) to find the optimum growing conditions.

4 THE TEMPLE OF PAN

There were many structures in the grounds of Osterley in the 18th century. It was fashionable to create an idealised landscape, dotted with romantic summerhouses and grottoes, and the family and their guests would spend fine summer days in leisure and pleasure out of doors. Sadly, some were temporary, and the Chinese tea-house and the windmill are now long gone. However, a delightful survival is the Temple of Pan, otherwise known as the Doric Temple. According to tradition, it was built in the 1720s by the architect John James of Greenwich; it certainly predates the Adam era. The interior contains fine rococo plasterwork.

THE ORANGERY

A more recent loss was Adam's large Doric Orangery, 27 metres (90 feet) long and 6 metres (20 feet) wide, constructed in 1763–4. It was known as the 'great green house' to distinguish it from the Garden House, but was destroyed by fire during the Second World War, when a blackout curtain was set ablaze by a stove.

Right The garden provides cut flowers to decorate the house

5 THE GREAT MEADOW

The Great Meadow lies to the west of the house, providing spectacular views from the Long Gallery. A large pedimented door opens from the gallery onto the elegant curving stairs, which give access to the grounds. In the 18th century, the estate was much larger than it is now. It was designed as a romantic landscape, with paths carefully laid out to offer vistas and glimpses of the 'ideal', framed by a wide variety of trees that were picked for their sculptural qualities and autumn colour.

The Great Meadow is a rare survival in Greater London; since Georgian times, it has never been ploughed, not even during the Second World War. Consequently, it is the ideal habitat for unusual wildflowers such as Lady's Bedstraw and Knapweeds, and rare insects such as orange-tipped butterflies and Burnet moths. From time to time the pastoral scene is enhanced by the presence of Charolais cattle, which belong to the tenant farmer, and are put into the Great Meadow for seasonal grazing.

6 THE LONG WALK

The Long Walk circles the Great Meadow and was designed as a path from which to admire the house. Today it runs through woodland which is being restored to its original state by removing imported shrubs and replanting native trees and flowers. Some of the viewpoints have also been re-created, offering stunning vistas. In the 18th century the Long Walk was more formal, with flowerbeds lining the path.

Opposite Cattle grazing the Great Meadow

Right The house from across the lake

7 THE LAKES

From many of the principal rooms in the house, it appears that a single, large expanse of water curves into the distance, but this is a carefully contrived illusion. There are in fact two separate lakes, but careful planting has made them appear as though they are continuous.

On one of the lakes is a boathouse, accessible by a flight of steps down to the water's edge. Servants would row guests around the waters on a variety of craft, including, at one stage, a Chinese sampan. The boathouse had been completely overgrown until it was cleared by volunteers, greatly improving the view back to the house.

8 THE ICE-HOUSE

Close to one of the lakes is a feature of 18th-century life which is now inaccessible to visitors. Beneath a large mound covered in mature trees is the ice-house, where servants would store ice retrieved from the lakes during winter. Before mechanical refrigeration the provision of ice was a great status symbol.

THE MAKERS OF OSTERLEY

Right The great financier Sir Thomas Gresham built Tudor Osterley

Below Tudor Osterley is shown on Moses Glover's 1635 map of Isleworth

TUDOR OSTERLEY

Sir Thomas Gresham (?1519–79) owned a farmhouse at Osterley, an area known for its fertility. Less than ten miles from the centre of London, the site was reasonably safe from the twin scourges of plague and politics. Wealthy and powerful, Gresham was a commercial adviser to the Crown; he owned much property, including a house in Antwerp, and he built a great townhouse for himself in Bishopsgate. On behalf of his only son, Richard, Thomas invested in Osterley, replacing the old farmhouse with a four-square, brick-built manor house complete with a central courtyard. He made the estate profitable by establishing one of the earliest paper mills in England. But Richard died in 1564, and although the following year he enclosed some 243 hectares (600 acres) of land around the farm, Thomas threw his energies into public projects. He underwrote the building of the Royal Exchange, based on the one in Antwerp. It was completed in 1568 and officially named by Queen Elizabeth in 1571.

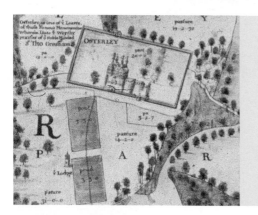

'... a faire and stately building of bricke, erected by Sir Thomas Gresham... and finished about 1577. It standeth in a parke by him also impaled, well wooded and garnished with manie faire ponds, which afforded not onely fish and fowle, as swannes, and other water fowle; but also great use for milles, as paper milles, oyle milles, and corne milles....'

John Norden, *Speculum Britanniae*, 1596.

An eventful royal visit

Elizabeth I visited Sir Thomas at Osterley at least twice, and stayed overnight at the house. Her visit in 1576 was eventful: two women tore up and burnt the fence and palings around the park, presumably in protest against Sir Thomas's enclosures a decade before. Elizabeth suffered 'great disturbance and disquiet'; never an easy guest, she also observed that the forecourt of the house was too large and would look better if it were divided by a wall. Bowing to regal authority, Sir Thomas ordered her whim fulfilled overnight, to the Queen's amusement.

THE STABLES

The Stables have been dated through dendrochronology to 1566, with further building work taking place in 1567/8. This massive building project is likely to have been undertaken by Gresham, either to impress Queen Elizabeth or to house her large household during her visits to Osterley.

Recent research has revealed that the Stables were much altered in the first few years after construction. This suggests that they were put up hurriedly, and had to be adapted even as they were being built to suit the needs of the estate.

The Stables were probably always intended to have many uses. As well as stabling, the Tudor building contained a very large barn in the east range for storing produce from the entire estate. The Stables have continued to be the 'engine room' of the estate. In 1714 the Child family added a clock-tower, and around that time converted the central range for stabling. The building has also accommodated a brewhouse, dairy, bakehouse, laundry and carriage-house in the 18th century, garages in the early 20th century, and visitor facilities today.

Below Tudor brickwork survives in the basement of the house

Below The Stables. The corner turret houses a spiral staircase

THE CHILD FAMILY

Francis Child (known as the Elder) was born in 1642 and apprenticed to a London goldsmith. He married Elizabeth Wheeler, daughter and sole heir of an established goldsmithing family. Banking, goldsmithing and property speculation made Francis Child rich – he became Lord Mayor of London, the MP for Devizes, and was well-connected to major figures of the day such as Sir Christopher Wren and John Evelyn.

In 1713 Francis acquired the manor house at Osterley in lieu of a mortgage owed to him by Dr Nicholas Barbon, who had died in debt. Gradual improvements were made by successive generations before Francis the Elder's grandson, also called Francis, engaged Robert Adam to remodel the house in 1761.

Francis died suddenly in September 1763, a week before his planned wedding. According to Horace Walpole, he left his fiancée a handsome legacy of £50,000. Francis left

Left Francis Child the younger, by Allan Ramsay

Right Robert Child, by Joshua Reynolds

Osterley to his brother Robert, who married Sarah Jodrell a fortnight later. Shortly afterwards, Robert commissioned Adam to create the interiors in the same Neo-classical style. Robert and Sarah lived here each year from May until November. They had a townhouse in highly fashionable Berkeley Square, and they also owned Upton House in Warwickshire, where they hunted.

The Child family were immensely rich. When Francis came into his inheritance in the 1750s, he was drawing between £4,500 and £7,800 a year from the business, an equivalent of £2–3 million today. Robert Child was entitled to 58% of the profits, and in 1768 he drew £13,000 – a vast sum, which was ploughed into remodelling Osterley in order to entertain his friends and family.

Robert Child forgave his errant daughter (see box), though the shock proved too much for him. He died alone in a seaside villa in Margate only two months after the elopement. But he had changed his will, and it was found that he had left Osterley (along with his vast fortune) to Sarah Anne's second child so long as he or she retained the surname Child. This was to prevent his family fortune falling into the hands of the Earls of Westmorland. Robert's widow Sarah took over the running of the estates and became a director of the bank. Nine years later, she remarried, to Lord Ducie, and continued to live with him at Osterley and Berkeley Square till her death in 1793.

Above The Earl of Westmorland

The runaway bride

Robert and Sarah's only child was called Sarah Anne. In 1782, at the age of 17, she eloped to marry John Fane, 10th Earl of Westmorland, whose nickname was 'Rapid Westmorland'. The Earl had asked Robert Child if he could marry his daughter, but he refused, possibly because of the Earl's reputation as a gambler. However, the Earl asked him, 'If you were in love with a girl and her father refused his consent, what would you do?' Robert replied, 'Why, run away with her, to be sure'. The Earl matched the word to the deed and eloped with Sarah Anne to Gretna Green in Scotland, with her family in hot but fruitless pursuit.

Right Sarah Anne Child as a girl

'... the palace of palaces ... so improved and enriched, that all the Percies and Seymours of Sion must die of envy.'

Horace Walpole, writing of Adam's changes to Osterley.

THE 19TH CENTURY

Sarah Anne's second child, Lady Sarah Sophia Fane, was born in 1785 and was only eight when she inherited Osterley and the Child family fortune in 1793. She married George Villiers (later Child-Villiers), 5th Earl of Jersey, in 1804, and the couple made his family home, Middleton Park in Oxfordshire, their country base. Their London home was the Childs' former town house, 38 Berkeley Square. The 5th Earl was a successful breeder and owner of racehorses, with three Derby winners. The extrovert Countess was a major player in London society, a leader of fashion, a supporter of Queen Caroline, and a friend and patron of Lord Byron. 'Queen Sarah', as she was known, was painted by Romney and Lawrence, and inspired the character of Zenobia in Disraeli's novel *Endymion*.

Even for the wealthy Jerseys, Osterley was expensive to maintain – £3,300 in 1812. The 5th Earl considered renting it out or even dismantling it, but fortunately the property remained in the family and passed to his son George Augustus Frederick, who died in 1859. The Dowager Duchess Sarah Sophia survived until 1867, but a tenant was found in the form of her first cousin, Grace Caroline, Dowager Duchess of Cleveland, who cared for the house until her death in 1883.

Margaret, wife of the 7th Earl, was crucial in securing the future of Osterley. She appreciated the beauty of Osterley and its historic function as a place for entertaining. A garden party held in 1884 was so successful with their guests that soon they were hosting Saturday-to-Monday parties at the property, with visitors ranging from princes and politicians to the landed aristocracy. The weekend house party became very popular with the Prince of Wales's set – he was later to become Edward VII. The house was lived in once more, even if only at weekends.

Difficult decisions were required to ensure its survival; to maintain the property and repair the roof, the family reluctantly decided to sacrifice the contents of the famous library, with its fifteen Caxtons. The eight-day sale in 1885 raised over £13,000, which paid for repairing the roof. The 7th Earl died in 1915, the 8th in 1923, when Osterley passed to the 9th Earl, George Francis Child-Villiers, who was then only thirteen.

Pride of the place

'... he turned back through the open doors into the great gallery which was the pride of the place. It marched across from end to end and seemed – with its bright colours, its high panelled windows, its faded flowered chintzes, its quickly-recognised portraits and pictures, the blue-and-white china of its cabinets and the attenuated festoons and rosettes of its ceiling – a cheerful upholstered avenue into the other century.'

Above The Long Gallery

Henry James (Summersoft in his 1888 novella, *The Lesson of the Master*, is based on Osterley).

46

THE 20TH CENTURY

In 1925 Lady Jersey, widow of the 8th Earl, remarried, and Lady Slesor (as she then was) brought in the Adam expert and curator of the Soane Museum, A.T. Bolton, to protect the integrity of the Adam rooms while electricity and central heating were installed. This enlightened and farsighted attitude ensured the survival of the house at a time when it could have been seriously damaged.

Despite its 'modern conveniences…and a museum collection of old pictures, furniture, tapestries, and objets d'art…' as advertised in *Country Life* in 1926, a suitable tenant could not be found for Osterley. In 1937–8, the Jersey family moved in while Middleton was being demolished and a new house being built in its place. Designed by Edwin Lutyens, Middleton Park was probably the last great country house to be built in England.

OSTERLEY AT WAR

George, 9th Earl of Jersey (1910–98) started opening the house to the public at Easter 1939, one of the first stately home owners to do so. He worked for Glyn Mills Bank, which had bought Child's Bank in 1924, and when World War II broke out, the firm moved part of its operations to Osterley for the duration.

Below The 9th Earl of Jersey; photographed by Bassano in 1931. He gave Osterley to the National Trust in 1949

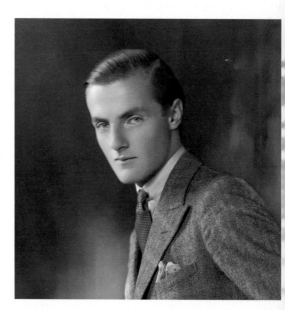

The 9th Earl also allowed the grounds to be used for the practical training of the Local Defence Volunteers, the forerunners of the British Home Guard. Led by the left-wing writer Tom Wintringham, the trainees were taught the theory and practice of modern warfare, from guerrilla tactics to house-to-house fighting, using some estate workers' houses scheduled for demolition.

The Surrealist artist Roland Penrose demonstrated camouflage painting techniques on the nude form of his mistress, the photographer Lee Miller; knife fighting and hand-to-hand combat were demonstrated by Bert 'Yank' Levy, a veteran of the Spanish Civil War, and the science of mixing homemade explosives was imparted by 'Mad' Major Wilfred Vernon, whose explosives store was located behind the Garden House. MI5 had their doubts about the 'bunch of socialist revolutionaries at the end of the Piccadilly Line', and after three months the War Office took charge, sending the staff and volunteers to three newly-opened official Home Guard schools. The park was largely given over to food production and ploughed up by the Land Girls, as part of the war effort.

When peace returned, the 9th Earl was insistent that this unique house, its setting and a large proportion of its contents should be preserved intact. In 1949 he gave the house and the grounds to the National Trust. They were subsequently leased out to the Ministry of Works, which maintained the property till 1991, when the Trust took over the running of Osterley. The furniture was purchased for the nation and placed in the care of the Victoria & Albert Museum, which later gave it to the Trust.

Below The training courses run for Local Defence Volunteers at Osterley in 1940 were publicised by *Picture Post*

PICTURE POST

CAMOUFLAGE
A Home Guard learns a lesson in cover at Osterley Park Training School.

HULTON'S NATIONAL WEEKLY
THE HOME GUARD CAN FIGHT
By TOM WINTRINGHAM
SEPTEMBER 21, 1940
Vol. 8. No. 12
3D

THE NATIONAL TRUST

The National Trust has to balance its commitment to public access with the long-term aim of conserving places of natural beauty and historical interest for future generations. The maintenance and care of each one of its hundreds of historic houses is a constant and unique challenge for the charity, and it seeks creative opportunities for houses to raise funds to support their maintenance. Osterley's magnificent interiors and proximity to London make it a frequently requested film and TV location: the Entrance Hall provided the setting for the ballroom scene in *The Duchess* (starring Keira Knightley), while scenes from *Miss Potter* (with Renée Zellwegger) and *Mrs Brown* (starring Judi Dench and Billy Connolly) were shot in the Long Gallery.

RESTORING OSTERLEY

The National Trust is currently implementing a large-scale restoration programme for the park and the garden. The park is currently used by 300,000 people a year, and many of them live locally. There are some 35,000 visitors a year to the house, and the interpretation of the property is constantly evolving, with the development of new exhibition rooms and the gradual re-instatement of the servants' quarters 'below stairs'. Osterley has a particular commitment to engaging with local communities, through initiatives such as *London Voices*, making urban families aware of the heritage on their doorsteps.

A PRECIOUS GREEN SPACE

As green spaces on the outskirts of cities come under increasing pressure from development, it is vital that unique survivals such as Osterley Park are protected for the future. There is also a duty of care for the wildlife which has made Osterley its home; species include barn owls, little owls, foxes, muntjac deer, bats and kingfishers. The lakes provide a safe habitat for newts, carp, mandarin ducks and Egyptian geese.

THANK YOU

Thank you for supporting the work of the National Trust by buying this guidebook. All of the profits, along with those from sales in our shop and tea-room and all admission fees, go directly to helping maintain Osterley Park and House.

Left The *London Voices* project: making the most of Osterley